THANK YOU!
YOU'RE WELCOME!

E. DELBERT GRAY, PhD

Wasteland Press
www.wastelandpress.net
Shelbyville, KY USA

Thank You! You're Welcome!
by E. Delbert Gray

First Printing – November 2011
ISBN: 978-1-60047-641-9

Cover photo: The deep pink rose is the only flower with "thank you" as its sole significance.
To submit your own personal appreciation and gratitude stories, please visit www.thankyouyouarewelcome.com or email the author at edg@thankyouyouarewelcome.com.
Cover photo credit: © Ksenya73 @www.dreamstime.com

Printed in the U.S.A.

0 1 2 3 4 5 6

DEDICATION

To the most encouraging and supportive people in my world who have helped to shape my life and career: you have inspired and helped me in so many ways. As my mother-in-law, Mrs. Eunice Robinson Sims, constantly said to me every time we saw each other, "I thank you, I love you, and I thank God for you." This book was inspired by each of you.

Dr. Sylvia Sims Gray, Brandon Bryant Gray, Ashley Alana Gray, Elisha Z. and Lavada E. Gray, Prudence Diane Hollins, Daniel Z. Gray, Phillip and Prudence Washington, Rev. Dr. Frank K. and Eunice R. Sims, Frankiee Sims Ervin, Eva Monday, Wilbur Higgins, Elisha and Alpina Gray, Percy Jones, Nute Williamson, Rev. Dr. Charles G. Adams, Dr. John W. Porter, Harry Lash, Robert Charles Mealing, Rev. Herman Griffin, Dr. Charles Blackman, Lawrence Doss, Governor William G. Milliken, Dr. Blanche Martin, Dr. Calvin Moore, James Ella "Granny" West, Earl and Gloria Powell, Dr. Helen Adams, Dr. Joseph Payne, Coach John Merritt, Dr. Leonard Slain, Dr. Thomas Gunnings, Dr. Charles Warfield, Dr. Charles Moody, Edgar Brazelton, Benjamin Bernoudy, Charlie Brown, Roy Levy Williams, Senator David Holmes, Neil Zalenko, John Barth, Bo Andersson, Bob Rossiter, and Elinor Josaitis.

ACKNOWLEDGMENTS

I wish to acknowledge and express my appreciation to all who shared their life space with me: my family, relatives, friends, associates, and colleagues, because you have made such profound difference to me.

I personally and professionally say thank you for the good times. Each one really played a part in developing me, for it is very real that the good times make one stronger.

I would also like to thank Susan Giffin for her contributions toward making this, my first book, a reality.

CONTENTS

FOREWORD

We thank God for many things, both great and small: the faithful fluctuations of the four seasons; the fruits, flowers, and gorgeous garniture of nature, the midnight stars and nourishing rain, for the bountiful harvest of golden grain, for those whom we love and by whom we are loved and encouraged, for the faces of friends, for the chuckles and laughter of precious infants, for the alert brilliance of children, for the astute thinking of adolescents, for the creative energy and critical alertness of young adults, the maturity of the middle-aged, and for the wise words and guiding influence of seasoned people who enrich our minds and secure our lives with their unconditional commitment to our fulfillment; for the past that secures, the present that excites and for the future that waits, for the spirituals that rock our souls, for the anthems that elevate our thoughts, for the hymns that heal our hearts, for the gospels that stimulate public and private worship, and for the "Messiah" by Handel, B Minor Mass by Bach, Beethoven's Ninth, and Stevie Wonder's "Happy Birthday" for "Caesar's hand and Plato's brain, for Lord Christ's heart and Shakespeare's strain"; for all these things and myriad more, we make our humble thanks to the Lord our God.

May we never cease to praise God, confess to God, thank God, and implore God's presence and peace, for only in commitment, consciousness, and service to God can we succeed in grace, suffer in hope, and live in victory daily. The writing of Paul the Apostle drips with the sweet unction and strong instruction of Philippians 4:11-13: "I have learned to be thankful whatever the circumstances (my translation). I know what it is to be in need, and I know what it is to have more than enough. I have learned the secret of being content in any and every situation, whether living in plenty or in want. I can do everything through him who gives me strength."

Giving thanks to God and people is drinking from the deepest well of generosity and joy. We are happiest and most generous when we feel, say, and exude gratitude. We are most miserable when we feel no impulse to express sincere thanks for all we have received. It is my great delight to thank God for the priceless treasure of having known a relative who was a mathematical genius, author, lecturer, poet, journalist, theologian, anthropologist, sociologist, pastor, professor, philanthropist, and humanitarian. He was Gordon Blaine Hancock (1884-1970). He was the epitome of all that I am and hope to be. It was he who taught me the profound value of the art of gratitude in acknowledgment of kindnesses received. He told me, "Nobody is worse than an ingrate." Ingrates are crude, thoughtless, and clueless.

Giving thanks is wise and rewarding. It reassures the giver; it positions the thankful soul to receive additional benefits; it improves the spirit; and it elevates the ethical character of the human community. Giving thanks presupposes the reality and the being of a great, generous Creator, Redeemer, and Restorer of human life. Gratitude is not a random shot in the dark of disbelief; it is a targeted expression of appreciation, directed to the Fountain of life and the Giver of every good and perfect gift. We believe that we owe thanks to God and to the children of God who love us and teach us.

When I was a college student at Fisk University, I requested of my grand uncle the money to buy something I did not need. He wrote back, “Dear Charles, I have no intention of robbing you of your greatest and most lasting satisfaction, namely, the struggle necessary to obtain your own education. I will send you no money at all, but I will pray that God will strengthen you to become an educated preacher and teacher. Love always, Gordon Blaine Hancock.”

I answered him immediately, “Dear Uncle Gordon, thank you for correcting my foolish request by teaching me value of self-help and self-reliance in the effort to become worthy of my calling to preach the Gospel. I will become a better person by your wise refusal to indulge my materialistic request. I intend to profit greatly from your tough love and tender heart. Gratefully yours, Charles.”

Twelve years later, when I was a graduate at the University of Michigan and Harvard Divinity School, and pastor of Concord Baptist Church, Boston, Massachusetts, I received a letter containing a considerable sum of money, saying, "Dear Charles, I am entrusting these funds to your care. I want you to educate your children, feed your congregation, and continue to develop your mind, heart, and spirit to the glory of God and the good of mankind. Love always, Uncle Gordon."

If I had been ungrateful for my uncle's discipline, I would have become ineligible for his huge trust, confidence, and benefaction. Heartfelt, habitual, and overflowing gratitude is good character, good religion, good business, and good senses. Be thankful for all things, most especially for the challenges, struggles, and tests of character that enrich our hearts, improve our personalities, and enhance human life on Earth.

"Thanks be to God for God's indescribable gift!" (2 Corinthians 9:15)

Rev. Dr. Charles G. Adams, 74
Senior Pastor
Hartford Memorial Baptist Church
Detroit, Michigan
&
Professor
Harvard Divinity School
Boston, Massachusetts

INTRODUCTION

I wish somebody would say "thank you."

Growing up on the east side of Detroit in the 1950s, I remember life was promising, something to be cherished. My life revolved around attending Sunday church services, being a vocal participant in very lively conversations at home, participating in Boy Scout activities, swapping stories with neighbors, playing sports, listening to good music, and simply enjoying life.

Being raised in a household with multiple generations – mother, father, grandmother, and great grandmother – contributed significantly to my love for people. There were family friends and relatives living in our home for short and long periods of time. Every day there was a lot of laughter, plenty of jokes and food, and my mother on the phone enjoying conversations with her cherished friends and club members. In every corner of my life, I saw people loving and appreciating each other.

Good manners were important in our home. "Please... Yes, ma'am... No, sir... Thank you... You're welcome" were modeled to my siblings and me and became a natural part of our active vocabulary.

As I grew older, I learned how much people appreciate being recognized for their good deeds. Something powerful happens to the giver, and to the receiver, when thankfulness is expressed. The power of these two words blesses us with peace and optimism, values others, and assures that no one is taken for granted.

From about the age of seven, I shined shoes in my dad's Family Barbershop, where stories were told so vividly, as if the storyteller was the original author. When I was old enough to cut hair and have my own barber chair, I learned the importance of good relationships with my customers: judges, ministers, lawyers, teachers, doctors, factory workers, and the corner philosopher. They had one thing in common: they enjoyed being recognized and appreciated. Most of them believed I was a good and loyal friend. I learned how to laugh at each of their jokes, and to give each customer their "propers." Every day, the barbershop was filled with words of appreciation, jokes, and stories loaded with life lessons.

The value of a good story with a message of appreciation stuck with me throughout the years, and the meaning of gratitude and appreciation instilled in me at an early age has never left me. I vividly remember how I felt when I said "thank you" to my great grandmother. It brought a smile to her face that made me feel warm inside, recognized, and loved; most importantly, she appreciated my words.

A story that means a great deal to me is one I've told a thousand times; it's the story of a young couple that lived in the South. The husband had only a seventh-grade education; his wife had completed only the ninth grade. They had five sons and lived on a farm of about ten acres. The father worked the land, harvested the produce, and sold it to support his family.

The mother became sick at a young age and died, but before she passed, she said to her husband, “Whatever you do, please make me one promise: you will do everything you possibly can to make sure all of our sons finish college.”

Well, their father not only made the promise but also kept his word. He got a job, in addition to working his own land, and he paid for a college education for his five sons. All of them secured good jobs working up North. They bought new cars, new homes, and the best of everything. They made a lot of money but only very, very infrequently returned to see their father. They were too busy with their own lives and families.

When their father died, they went home to bury him. They tried to show the community how much they loved their father, so they booked the largest church and the most popular preachers. They bought all the flowers they could find in town, secured the finest mortician to do his best work on their father, and bought the most expensive casket. They let everyone in the community know about the funeral and said they would feed everyone afterward at the church.

As the service was underway, the church was packed. All of a sudden an old lady entered the sanctuary. She was ragged in her appearance. She carried a large covered pot with towels and rags wrapped around it, but steam was still escaping. People at the back of the church motioned for her to leave, but the oldest brother saw the disturbance and said, "Hold it. Maybe she has something to say." So, the old woman continued walking up the aisle. When she reached the front of the sanctuary, the older son said, "Pardon me, ma'am, but what is in the pot you're carrying?"

"In my hands," she said, "I have the soup your father loved for me to make him. It's my famous chicken noodle soup."

"Listen," the elder son said, "do you understand that this is a funeral? Our father is dead. He can't smell or taste your chicken noodle soup."

The old woman looked at him and said, "Son, if your father can see and smell all those flowers you bought to fill the church, he can surely smell and taste my chicken soup."

The moral of this story is to express our feelings of appreciation NOW to our loved ones while they can still appreciate them.

How many funerals have we attended where we found daughters, sons, family, and friends cry out that they never told their deceased loved one that they loved, appreciated, and honored them? How many times have we missed opportunities to let someone know how much we appreciate them before it was too late? How many teachers have made a difference in our lives, but we forgot to tell them?

As a challenged student, I knew I needed to recognize the teachers who helped me. Mrs. Calvert, for instance, constantly shook her head whenever I produced a jumble of work. Her dismay became patience when I would say, "Thank you, Mrs. Calvert, for helping me." I wanted her to know how much I appreciated her patience.

Teachers, mentors, coaches, tutors, and principals plant seeds of faith, inspiration, and hope in each of us. Expressing our appreciation is the least we can do in return.

When I began my career as a teacher and administrator, I never stopped showing appreciation to others. I knew that prayer and words of encouragement had brought me through difficult times. I never forgot to express gratitude for the many blessings and acts of kindness others have bestowed on me: those who helped me to become who I am, on whose shoulders I stood – and still stand – as I strive to make a difference and to support others in their pursuit of educational and business opportunities.

In today's fast-paced world, we are moving away from expressing our appreciation when someone opens a door for us or when we receive a lovely gift or excellent service, or when an employee makes a significant contribution to our business.

I remember calling an employee on their private cell phone and saying, “Thank you for being part of our company. You are without question a very important employee, and you have added value to our company. Welcome to our family.” A phone call like that would change the mindset of almost any employee, because employers definitely cannot pay what employees are worth, but EVERY employer can take a moment and say “thank you” to enhance morale and show respect and appreciation.

When we don’t express appreciation, is it because we are in an empty place? Are our minds on other things so much in our race to move up that we forget those who helped get us moved up the ladder? Are we so preoccupied with our hand-held devices or computers that making direct contact with others takes too much effort? Have our hurt feelings from the past not healed or do we feel blocked from recognizing the goodness of others in our life? Does anxiety, stress, or negativity contribute to any emptiness we feel?

The appreciation of a “thank you” connects generations. I certainly would enjoy receiving a letter telling me how wonderful my mom or dad was or thanking our family for sharing such wonderful folks with them. It’s good to know that gratitude is included in our DNA. Hearing about an encouraging word that our parents said to someone or a kind gesture that they extended in an hour of despair gives us a measure of happiness too.

Life gives us several roads on which to travel. From my view, the first road on life's journey is **mindfulness.** It is imperative that we keep track of how blessed and gifted we are; how important our family, friends, and loved ones are; and how special the efforts of our teachers, youth, community leaders, and ministers are to our lives.

The second road is the ability to **acknowledge one's personal and professional development.** This road allows us to become who we are, and inclines in the road help us to build careers and businesses and bless us with opportunities to care for our family, friends, associates, and employees. Acknowledging our personal and professional development allows the enhancement of our life through the support of the lives of others.

The third road is the open space along life's highway called **return.** Returning the blessings one has received and providing blessings for others. Returning to say thank you, to let those who helped you know how much you appreciate their assistance as you move toward your destination.

Little gestures can turn into life-altering moments on life's journey. What goes around comes around in the form of grace, thanksgiving, and generosity of spirit. On a daily basis, we have opportunities to show our appreciation for the blessings we receive.

I'm reminded of the story of a newly arrived soul in heaven. St. Peter met him at the gate and showed him around heaven. They walked side by side inside a large workroom filled with angels.

St. Peter stopped in front of the first section and said, "This is the receiving section. All petitions to God said in prayer are received here." The soul looked around and saw that it was terribly busy with so many angels sorting out petitions written on volumes of paper from all the people of the world.

They walked again until they reached the second section, and St. Peter told him, "This is the packaging and delivery section. Here the graces and blessings people asked for are packed and delivered to them down on Earth."

The soul saw how busy this department was. There were so many angels working, getting blessings ready to be delivered to Earth.

Finally, in the farthest corner of the room, the soul stopped. To his surprise, there was only one angel in that section, sitting idle, doing nothing. "This is the acknowledgment section," said St. Peter.

"How is it that there is no work here?"

"That is the sad thing," St. Peter answered. "After people receive the blessings they asked for, very few send their acknowledgments."

"How does one acknowledge God's blessings?"

"Simple," St. Peter answered. "Just say, thank you, Lord."

God placed this book on my heart. After accepting His direction, I proceeded to develop what could be a transformative gift to those who read it as well as to those who contributed to it. The material is original from the authors, including family members and friends who understand and appreciate gratitude. They enthusiastically seized the opportunity to search their own hearts and minds for the meaning of gratitude and the desire for harmony as they extended appreciation to people who were the guiding lights in their lives. Each person has been blessed with the ability to draw upon wisdom, love, and deep gratitude. This anthology – a collection of stories, poems, testimonials, and essays – reflects the point where each writer felt compelled to write an expression. These contributions are highly personal and reflective.

My hope is that you will feel the value of thankfulness and its transformative power. Our world will be impacted by our return of gratitude in such a positive way.

Reading this book will inspire you, move you to tears, and bring a chuckle or two. Most of all, you will be reminded that we truly matter to each other.

I want to reinstate gratitude in our lives and our world and to refrain from taking kind gestures for granted. Our own happiness is in direct proportion to the love and thankfulness we express to others.

–E. Delbert Gray, PhD

NOTE: At the end of each chapter, there are questions or suggestions to prompt you to explore the implications of the entries in your own life, as well as to raise questions about what you may have taken for granted, but how you now know to reach out and express your thanks.

PART I
SPIRITUALITY

If we overlook gratitude, it will be at our own emotional and psychological peril.

Rev. Peter Gomes

Howard Thurman, in his work entitled, A Litany of Thanksgiving, writes, "Today, I make a sacrament of thanksgiving, in being with the simple things of my days: fresh air to breathe, cool water to drink, the taste of food, the protection of houses and clothes, the comforts of home. For these, I make an act of thanksgiving this day!"

IT'S TIME TO COUNT OUR BLESSINGS

Whether it's Thanksgiving Day or not, we should focus on one powerful phrase: "I thank you." It should always be on the tip of our tongue if we are truly grateful to others who help us each day, and to God who has richly blessed us with more abundance and freedom than any country in history.

Despite God's abundant blessings, we're often too slow to give thanks and too quick to complain. Maybe we're so focused on ourselves and busy with our lives that we forget to give thanks. Or maybe we in America have become complacent with a level of luxury and leisure beyond the imagination of much of the world's population.

We tend to take our blessings for granted, like the homeowner who hired a real estate agent to prepare an ad to sell his home. The homeowner read the ad in the paper about his home's many attractive features. He called the real estate agent to say he no longer wished to sell. When asked what changed his mind, the homeowner said, "After reading your ad, I realized I already live in the house I always wanted to live in."

Even if it's not Thanksgiving, it's always time to count our blessings and pull out that simple phrase, "I thank you."

Rich DeVos, 85

International Commodities Business Owner

WITH ANOTHER DAY

Because of my life experiences, I am thankful for every day. I choose to see the glass as half full, instead of half empty. I say this, because I lost both my sisters to breast cancer. My youngest sister died at thirty-seven years; my next sister at forty-eight. My father died at sixty-one of colon cancer, and my stepson at twenty-five of kidney disease. I have survived breast cancer twice. I don't ask why me, but why *not* me.

Rather than becoming bitter, I have been thankful for the time and relationships I had with my family. I am fortunate, because they were all good. While I miss them terribly, I was blessed to have had them in my life. My father was my best friend; I could share anything with him. My sisters and I had a history together that no one else could have had. I miss our girls' day out. I considered my stepson my own son. I was his mom and his only caregiver during his years of illness.

These experiences taught me how little we need to make it in this world. Look around you. Our needs are being met; our wants are what we fret over. Every day is a good day. It is not dependent on the weather, how much money I have, if I have a job, or if I have what I want to eat. It is a good day, because God in His mercy and grace has allowed me to wake up, have the use of my mind and limbs, and a desire to make this a better world. No matter what happens today, if I go to sleep tonight and am blessed to get up tomorrow, I will have an opportunity to make this day better than yesterday.

I say "Thank you, God" many times a day, and He says, "You are welcome" by showing me His mercy and blessing me with another day.

Brenda Gibson Johnson, 64
Retired Business Manager

OH, GIVE THANKS

Oh, give thanks to the Lord, for He is good. *–Psalms 136:1*

We give thanks because He is good, and everything that came from Him is good. When we say thanks, we are giving thanks for good deeds that have been done. Everything good that mankind does is because of the goodness of God in him. Every good and perfect gift comes from above and comes down from the Father of Lights, with whom there is no variation or shadow of turning.

We should give thanks because His mercy endures forever.

Oh, give thanks to the God of Gods. *–Psalms 136:2*

We should give thanks because there is no other God like the God of Gods. He spoke the universe into existence, from which the complete system of all things exists. There is nothing lacking for all things to function in the way He intended.

He alone, with wisdom, has given mankind all things to enjoy in the universe, and His delight is with the sons of men.

We should give thanks because His mercy endures forever.

Oh, give thanks to the Lord of Lords. *–Psalms 136:3*

He is Lord over all aspects of life, and it does not matter about the circumstances you may face. He is Lord over it.

There were 10 men who were lepers, and they lifted up their voices and said, “Jesus, Master, have mercy on us.” So when He saw them, he told them to go and show themselves to the priest. He healed all 10 at one time. Master means chief commander. They knew that Jesus was in total command of disease and death, and they trusted Him to help them. The Samaritan leper understood that the Master was Lord of Lords, and His mercy endures forever.

Only one of the 10 men who were healed of leprosy returned to give thanks to the Master for healing him. He had a heart of gratitude. Every child of God should cultivate the grace of gratitude. It opens the heart to further blessings, and also glorifies and pleases the Father. The unthankful heart is fertile soil for all kinds of unlawful things.

Oh, give thanks to the God in Heaven. *–Psalms 136:26*

Our focus should be on giving thanks to God for who He is and for what he has done for His people. God, in His mercy, does not give us what we deserve, and by His grace, He gives us what we do not deserve. We should give thanks to our Lord God because He remembered us in our lowly state.

If we are truly thankful for our daily bread and acknowledge that God provides it, then we are not likely to turn away from Him and worship other gods. The creatures of Earth look to God for their needs and show their thanks by obeying His will and giving glory to Him.

If we think more about the goodness of God and His mercy, we will be apt to give more thanks for all He has done. Oh, give thanks to the God of Heaven, for His mercy endures forever.

Winford Bailey, 66
Entrepreneur

A PRECIOUS GIFT FROM GOD

Thank you, Lord, for my little understanding of life. Thank you, God, for letting me know that this minute, this hour, and this day is a precious gift from you. Thank you, God, for giving me parents who loved me every day of my life.

Thank you, God, for my sister who, through her presence (sibling rivalry), gave me my competitive spirit to finish high school and college. Thank you, God, for my soul mate, wife and best friend, for allowing us to travel life's journey together for more than thirty-eight years without losing an ounce of lust, love, and respect for each other. Thank you, God, for giving me the vision to recognize her profound value far beyond her initial earth-shaking sex appeal. Thank you, God, for allowing me to come to the understanding that real love goes beyond the bedroom.

Real love is the main ingredient of every meal prepared in the kitchen of life. Thank you, God, for giving me the understanding to know the difference between fast food and soul food. One is prepared with love from life's kitchen; both can taste good, but only one goes beyond the tongue and satisfies the spirit and soul.

Thank you, God, for giving me the blessing of my son and daughter. I believe when you have one of each, you have everything the baby store has to offer. Both of them have provided more joy than I could ever express. Thank you for allowing me the pleasure of watching them to grow, graduate, and mature. Their births forced me to change my focus from me to them.

Thank you, God, for giving me just a little insight into the responsibility you must feel for all of us. Thank you for giving me the ability and desire to provide for my wonderful family. Thank you, God, for giving me a few special friends and role models along my journey.

Bill Harris, 60
Packaging Business Owner

QUESTIONS & SUGGESTIONS

1. As you observe and listen to your family, friends, and others talk about their various concerns and issues, you shake your head or walk away and say, "Wow!" Ask yourself, "When was the last time I thanked God for what He has NOT put me through?"

2. Just think about the blessings that have been bestowed upon you. Start the practice of writing down your blessings each day. Share your list with a friend and, when times get hard, reflect on your list of blessings.

PART II

GRATITUDE TO FAMILY & FRIENDS

Be thankful for what you have;
You'll end up having more.

Oprah Winfrey

We have many reasons to thank members of our family and our close circle of friends who, on a regular basis, extend courtesies, services, and kindnesses to us, often without expecting anything in return.

THE GREATEST GIFT ANY CHILD CAN GIVE A PARENT

After spending a delightful weekend with my eighteen-year-old daughter, I was returning her to her college dorm. While I was driving, she was typing a paper due the following Monday. She looked up and, with a serene smile, said, "Thank you, Mom. Thank you." Thinking she was referring to our weekend, I remarked, "I'm glad you enjoyed the weekend."

She clarified her remark by stating that she was thanking me for being the parent I was, and for helping her to become the person she was becoming.

A few Sundays later, as my pastor dedicated two infants, he stated that the greatest gift any child can give a parent is to say "thank you." My heart swelled with pride and joy, as I reflected on my daughter's remarks.

Thank you...you're welcome: such simple words with such power – the power to turn a bad day into a good one, a frown into a smile, an acquaintance into a friend. These little words give validation to the giver as well as to the receiver. When you say "thank you," you acknowledge that you are valued enough to be the recipient of someone's kindness.

When the giver replies with "you are welcome," he affirms that you received his action with appreciation.

When we continually express our appreciation to others, our relationships are improved. We are viewed as thoughtful, considerate, and appreciative. People experience an increase in the frequency of acts of kindness, deliberate, or random.

We begin teaching our children at very young ages to say "thank you" and "you're welcome." It begins as a rote process. As our children age and mature, the action should become a meaningful and thoughtful expression of appreciation. This will occur as they observe us put these words into action. With increased frequency in hearing, expressing, and receiving these words, our children's self-esteem will be significantly enhanced. They will be more motivated to reach out to help others and to feel good about the effort that they put forth.

Catherine Hyde's book, Pay It Forward, stresses the importance of expressing "thank you" and "you're welcome" by performing acts of kindness to others. The concept of "pay it forward" involves repaying a good deed done to you with a good deed to a third party. When the third party asks how he can pay you back, you tell him to help someone else in need, or "pay it forward."

Ralph Marston, editor of the *Daily Motivator*, best sums it up. "Make a habit to tell people thank you; express your appreciation sincerely and without the expectation of anything in return. Truly appreciate those around you, and you'll soon find many others around you. Truly appreciate life, and you'll find that you have more of it." It's a win-win situation.

Beverly Parker Lewis, PhD, 62
Licensed Clinical Psychologist

MY FIRST UNDERSTANDING

As it is with most, my first understanding of "thank you" was taught by my parents to my siblings and me. It was taught as an appropriate gesture when receiving something from someone and was usually followed by a "you're welcome." Thank you was definitely a mandate for us outside the house, among other family members and friends when we received a compliment, pleasant exchange, gift, or gesture.

When occasionally we forgot this offer of gratitude, our parents quickly reminded with the words, "What do you say?" Momma and Daddy taught us by example; they always displayed an "attitude of gratitude" for the many blessings we had, both tangible and otherwise.

Today, as a married father of three, I take great strides to give my children the understanding of thanksgiving that was given to me. We start and end each day thankfully kneeling before God the Father, giving thanks for all that He has done, all that He is doing, and all that He is going to do. I believe if we kneel before the Father in the morning and give thanks, we can stand in the company of any man or woman during the day, ready to share the power of gratitude.

Let us remember to say "thank you" and "you're welcome." It truly is the gift that keeps on giving.

Thank you, God the Father, and Mom and Dad for a lifelong understanding of this most precious consideration. I will do all that I can to pass it on to my children and to others.

Al Horton, 49
Business Development Planner

CROSSROADS OF LIFE

Why say thank you? Well, being blessed with loving parents, great upbringing, educational experiences second to none, and exceptional life choices, why *not* say thank you? For when discussing life with others and learning of their experiences, you find it is indeed a blessing to have encountered what you have and how you withstood the challenges and roadblocks to become who you have become.

So, I say thank you to my loving parents and siblings, my devoted teachers, my caring neighbors, my wonderful and supportive friends, my physicians and dentists, my tennis and golf pros, my spiritual counselors, and my special relationship with my Father Lord in Heaven, for none of this would have been possible without His blessings.

For none of us has control of what family we are born into and where, but after living and experiencing the many crossroads of life, you learn that where you come from and how you develop from that deserves many thanks. The paths we sometimes choose to travel are not always the best of choices, and the consequences turn out to be not so pleasant and favorable, but through perseverance, love and intelligent redirection of your path, you resurface a better human being that can and does make a difference. That doesn't deserve a thank you?

Let us not forget our own effect on our life travels by saying thank you. Just think how you feel when you are told you are appreciated by the words “thank you.” The sincerity of that statement alone is so powerful. Look at the smile and the change of one’s disposition, when you say thank you for their work or service, friendship or love. This affirmation in saying “thank you” is and always will be a mandate for true relationships. So, I say thank you!

Kenneth E. Harris, 55
Business Consultant

MAMA SACRIFICED HERSELF

Love of God, family and our fellowman was always the focal point in everything we did. I thank them for instilling values in my sister and me that have served us well over the years. Moral and Christian standards, the value of education, a sense of self-esteem, respect for others, the value of friendships, work ethics, and a love for the arts were taught to us not only through words, but also through deeds and actions. We learned that even though our earthly father had died, we had a father in heaven that cared for us, and that being impoverished financially does not have to make you impoverished spiritually and emotionally. I remember the Bible verse Mama always recited as we sat down to our meal: "All things work together for the good of them that love the Lord and are called according to His purpose."

My mother did not just send us to church, she took us to church. She did not just tell us to pray, she knelt with us each night as we said our prayers. Bible study was routine, and even though resources were meager, sacrifices were made to afford music and dance lessons for us. I wondered, as a child, why Mama wore hosiery with runs in them; but, I now know she sacrificed herself for our betterment.

Poetry was read and recited by my mother, and trips to museums, concerts, the Jaberwocks, and plays were given to us by my grandmother. These women perpetuated in us a need for a certain refinement in life and to set lofty goals.

I felt privileged to sit with my grandmother, as she related information about my grandfather, a Methodist minister, telling stories of the churches he built in Ohio and Canada, my great grandmother and grandfather, and followed her side of my family back as far as slavery. I am grateful that my mother, having come from a privileged background, acquired graces that she was able to pass on.

What a wonderful childhood you provided for us. Thank you. I hope, in some small way, we have been able to carry on the legacy you left us by imparting these same values in our children.

Prudence Charleen Greene-Washington, 84
Retired Affirmative Action Director

CLEAN UP THE MESS

One day I made some soup for my two-year-old grandson. He started eating it by saying thank you. It caught me by surprise. I really wasn't paying attention to him, but someone told me, "The baby is talking to you." So I turned around and told him thank you and resumed my work, because I was not used to people saying thank you while they were eating. Most of the time, you cook, and people eat, and then get up and go about their business. The only way you know that they enjoyed it is because they eat it all up.

But, the baby said thank you. When I turned back around, he started to eat with his hands, putting cornbread into his soup and making a mess. It must have been good to him, because he starting talking to me again, "Love you." Now, that did something to me! I can see why He is a selfish God that loves to be praised, because that "Love you" made me feel pretty good.

The baby's parents started to tell the baby to sit down, because he was making a mess, but I looked at him and said, "Don't worry about it. I will clean up the mess."

I was just wondering: if I told God thank you and let Him know that I loved Him, would He clean up the mess? If I told God "Thank you for the job that you gave me," would He clean up the mess? If I told God "thank you for the house that you gave me," would He clean up the mess?

See, “thank you” got my attention, but “Love you” got my reaction.

Edward Smith, 55
Machinist

A CHILD'S LESSON

I arrived in Southfield, Michigan, from Indianapolis to visit my sister and her family. I was anxious to see my little niece and nephew, Ashley and Brandon. I had no children of my own, so they were like my own children.

At the time of my arrival, Ashley, who was two years old, was home; her brother was at a friend's house. I couldn't wait until Brandon returned home to pass out the gifts I had brought, especially when Ashley rushed over to give me a big hug and said, "Aunt Frankiee, I love you so much." As I started to melt with pride, I said, "Ashley, I have a gift for you." I handed her a beautiful package tied with a big bow.

Ashley quickly opened the package and found an adorable Teddy bear. "Oh, Aunt Frankiee, thank you, thank you, thank you!" After few minutes, Ashley ran off with her new Teddy bear.

Shortly, she returned and said, "Aunt Frankiee, I think you forgot something."

I said, "Did I forget something? Is there something wrong with the Teddy bear?"

"You know, Aunt Frankiee, you know. You know what you forgot."

"No, I don't."

Ashley had such a serious look on her face. "Aunt Frankiee, you know what you forgot."

I looked at my sister, “Do you know what I forgot?”

She said, “I don’t know.”

Ashley finally said, “You know, Mommy and Daddy taught me that when someone says thank you, you are supposed to say you’re welcome.”

“Thank you, Ashley. I apologize.”

Frankiee Sims Ervin, 66
Retired Speech and Language Pathologist

I HEARD HER WORDS

One very memorable experience to me is my mother thanking me for having the courage and conviction at the age of seventeen in the late 1960s to attend college out of town. I did it in spite of lacking any financial resources from home; being uncertain about receiving a financial aid package to cover my first-year tuition; living away from home for the first time at a place I had never before visited; and having to overcome academic deficiencies by taking proficiency classes to meet freshman grade level standards.

Having attended Lewis Business College in Detroit in the 1940s, my mother was aware of the many academic obstacles I had to overcome, and the amount of effort I had to put forth to graduate from Wilberforce University in 1970 with a 3.8 cumulative grade point average.

My mother, not having a dependable family vehicle, took the bus to Wilberforce to attend my graduation. After the ceremony, she told me she was so proud of what I had accomplished. I appreciated her comments but in the excitement of the moment, I continued to celebrate with the other graduates.

Many years later, in fact a few months before my mother passed away in 1999, she talked about my graduation from college and what that meant to our family. As I was her first child to receive undergraduate and graduate degrees from several universities, she thanked me for creating the momentum for my younger brothers, sister, and even my own children to attend college. She further told me that because of me, our family would be stronger and wiser in generations to come.

My mother's kind words of thanks contributed greatly to my success in corporate America by giving me the confidence and self-esteem to accomplish many of my goals. Her words of thanks will always resonate in my heart and remind me that I should communicate thanks to my family for their accomplishments.

Eddie Floyd, 63
Retired Automobile Industry Executive

HE BELIEVED IN ME

My father was a hardworking family man who was committed to taking care of the ungrateful house full of children that he came home to every night. Though we knew he loved us, there was nothing warm and fuzzy about my father; he was a tough love kind of guy.

In 1980, I approached my father with an idea for a business venture that I had been waiting for. I have always had an entrepreneurial spirit, so it was quite common for me to share ideas with my family. This idea was different, however. I knew I could make it work, because I had the drive and commitment to do so. I lacked a key component – the money to fund it. Only one person in the world would even consider giving me the kind of money I needed.

My father had spent thirty-three years working for Chrysler, so he was definitely from the old school: you go to work, get a check, retire, and still get a check. He knew my spirit and my work ethic, but more than that, he believed in me. So when I pitched my business idea to him, after much consideration he agreed to lend me $13,000, his entire life savings.

A commitment to hard work, perseverance, integrity, blessings from God, and a little luck have allowed me to build a successful career, which has afforded me to not only take care of my family but also to give back to the community.

I often wonder where I would be and what I would be doing if my father had not had the faith in me to support me over thirty years ago. My dad, Charlie James Grant, Sr., died sixteen years ago. I said it then, and I will say it again. To you, my father, who loved and believed in me, THANK YOU!

Charlie James Grant, Jr., 57
Transportation Business Owner

ONE DAY AFTER MY BIRTH

In reflecting on my childhood, I must give honor to George and Clara Price, whom God charged to nurture, guide, teach, and direct me in my development.

After my high school graduation, I realized how blessed I was. It dawned on me that because of my parents and their love, I had never seen the inside of a jail.

In January 1963, I entered the U.S. Air Force. Before my departure, I sat down with my parents and told them how much I appreciated them. It was then that they told me that I was not their biological son. They had adopted me one day after my birth.

God had already ordained what my life would be. So, the final words at that moment were, "Thank you, Mom and Dad."

"You're welcome, son."

Bishop George W. Price, Jr., 67
Pastor

BRIGHTEN MY DAY

For me, a simple thank you from my children for little or big things I have done for them brightens my day, knowing that they appreciate what we are doing and don't take things for granted.

When I personally handed out bonus checks during the Christmas party, the gratitude and thanks I received really warmed my heart and made me more determined to do it again the following year.

I started the auto parts plant in Honduras in 2004, and during my first visit, 250 workers were so grateful for having jobs, they stood in line and thanked me, one by one. In some cases, they asked if they could hug me to thank me. It warmed my heart.

When my father had a stroke, the doctors informed us that he would not last through the night. We prayed for a miracle. God blessed us, and my father lived for another ten years. My mother converted to Christianity as a result, and I thank the Lord for that.

I thank the Lord every day for blessing me with the day, no matter how hard or blessed it was.

Hal Zaima, 60

International Business Owner

WHEN IT RAINS, SOMETIMES IT POURS

The year 1974 was very challenging for me, for it was a year of triumph and tragedy. I was a sophomore at Oakland University, and things were moving along pretty well. I was the student manager of the university's catering service, president of the Association of Black Students, a member of the University Student Congress, and my grades, although not Phi Beta Kappa status, were decent. I enjoyed the friendship and respect of my student colleagues, as well as many faculty, staff, and administrators. For all practical purposes, life was good.

One evening, after leaving a strategy session with the resident hall council, a storm began brewing in my life. Some students informed me that my brother was looking for me. Everywhere I went, the message was the same: "Have you seen your brother? He's looking for you." Finally, I arrived in my room, where my brother and two friends from the neighborhood were waiting for me.

The fact that they were in my room, which had been locked, led me to believe something serious had happened. My brother informed me that a relative in Ohio had passed and that my father had sent him to bring me home. It didn't make sense, but I packed a few clothes and headed home. Upon arriving, I learned the truth: my mother had been killed in a car accident. This was major for me. This was the first time in my entire life that anyone close to me died, but it didn't stop there. Two weeks later, after I returned to school, my father suffered a stroke. He was only fifty years old. The following week, his father passed away, and one week later, my father died. I lost two parents and a grandfather in thirty days, and all I could think of was when it rains, sometimes it pours. It was the first time in my life that I felt like I might lose my sense of direction and purpose.

That was when I learned that when it seems that you are at your worst, God is at His best. I returned to school, and the rain continued to pour. I was notified that I needed to pay a bill from the previous semester, or the university was going to cancel my registration and I would have to leave.

I did not know then that Dr. Manuel Pierson, Dean of Students, had become aware of my plight and was moving behind the scenes on my behalf. He contacted the director of financial aids and asked her if she might assist. In addition, he called a friend, Robert Shannon, a deacon at Tabernacle Missionary Baptist Church, a very prominent church in Detroit, and a member of the scholarship committee.

Robert Shannon pleaded my case to the committee. The irony of it all is that I had never met Mr. Shannon, even though I was good friends with his youngest son, also a student at Oakland University. Mr. Shannon convinced the committee to award its scholarship for that year to me, a non-member of the church. What a gracious act of mercy and a humbling experience for me!

My blessings did not stop there. I was informed the next day that Ms. Gladys Rappaport, Financial Aid Director, had decided to award me a scholarship given in honor of her work with students to use at her discretion. To this day and every day, I remain grateful to her for and humbled by the kindness and caring of people. What a powerful force that can be!

So, I would just like to say thank you. Thank you, Manuel Pierson, for the way you moved quietly behind the scenes to ease my burden at a time when I could not do it. Thank you, Robert Shannon, for your action and advocacy on behalf of a young man in need. Thank you, Gladys Rappaport, for caring enough to take a chance on me, as I realize there were countless students, equally in need of financial support and some more academically deserving.

Finally, I would like to thank God Almighty, who looked beyond my faults and saw my need and made it possible for me to complete my studies, and for instilling in me a heart to serve others.

Robert Thornton, 57
Grant Maker, Advocacy Foundation

I AM ALWAYS HERE

I remember as a young child feeling safe in the company of my Aunt Francis. I recall the fear and hopelessness of living at home, the long nights, hearing the loud rumblings of my parents. I longed to sleep through a weekend night in peace. I lived with my Aunt Francis on many occasions. I will always remember the long, fun nights of cleaning fresh smelt, eating fried green tomatoes, and bread and onion sandwiches. My Aunt Francis could create from leftovers a meal fit for a king.

Holidays and day-to-day living around Aunt Francis always made me feel happy and safe. As a young man, when life collided with my confidence, careers, and worthiness, I could call on my Aunt Francis at any hour of the night. She slept most of the day and spent long hours at night working on taxes for her customers, all the while dispensing wisdom in her conversations.

My Aunt Francis was and still is my greatest cheerleader, second only to my wife of twenty-five years and our two children. Now, at the age of nearly half a century, I still visit my Aunt Francis. She always told me "I am always here."

Aunt Francis, you will always be in my heart, and I love you much. You are the person that everyone wants to be around, the person that never changed, the person that I could go to for support, the mother that made me who I am today.

Jeffery Patton, 49
Bank Executive

THANK YOU FOR PLAYING YOUR ROLE

When I was a little boy, I could always count on my grandmother, Hazel Ferguson, to comfort me. I remember coming in from my morning paper route, and she would rub my hands together to get them warm, or make some hot chocolate. She lived with us until her death in 1960, when I was seventeen and a junior in high school.

My grandmother had more wise sayings than Confucius, even though she did not have a high school diploma. One day I was very upset with my dad for not buying me the shoes I wanted. My grandmother put her arms around me and said, "...I cried because I had no shoes, until I saw a man who had no feet." She always had a way of making me feel better, regardless of the situation. The phrase that served as the catch-all was "and this too shall pass." Of course, she was right. Thank you, Grandma Ferguson.

My mother was the ultimate multi-tasker. My older brother and sister and I were all in diapers at the same time. I don't know how she was able to keep us all clean and dry; there were no Pampers back then!

She also had to wash clothes, hang them out to dry, iron them, clean the house, and cook. She was an outstanding cook. We were poor and on a limited budget, and we didn't always have meat for dinner. My favorite meat-less meal, at least once a week, was northern white beans, stewed tomatoes, applesauce, and homemade cornbread. Mom also made the best rolls I have ever tasted. One of my friend's favorite Christmas gifts was a dozen of my mother's dinner rolls, even after he moved out of state. Thank you, Mother.

My dad told me that he was not trying to be my friend. My friends were the guys I played with. Dad's job was to be my dad. He had a strong work ethic and often worked overtime (for the City of Detroit, driving a bus or heavy equipment for the Sanitation Department), especially when it snowed. He didn't believe in giving us an allowance.

When I left the field of education and joined Ford Motor Company, my dad gave me one piece of advice: "I don't care how far you go with Ford, if you don't reach back and help some others you will have accomplished nothing." At one point in their lives, all of my brothers and one of my sisters worked for Ford. When I was the retired coordinator of affirmative action programs for Ford Motor Credit Company, I was able to help many minorities and women. They owe my dad a thank you, as well. Thank you, Dad.

I painted houses, including one for my next door neighbor, Mrs. Genevieve Francis. She was my best-paying paper route customer. Mrs. Francis went to a historically black college and was the first person I knew who had a college degree. She was always willing to help me with any of my school projects. Thank you, Mrs. Francis.

My next thank you is to Ms. Horner, my freshman English professor. She was known as the "black widow," not because her husband died (she never married), but because she was deadly when it came to freshmen in her English class. I grew to love and respect her. She was not only the best English teacher I had but also the best teacher I have ever had. She taught me to push myself beyond what I thought I could achieve. Thank you, Ms. Horner.

My last thank you goes to my wife of forty-six years, Kay D. Armstrong. She deserves many thanks. She's my corporate financial officer (CFO), housekeeper, interior decorator, mother of our two sons, grandmother to our three grandchildren, and lead shopper. I met her while we were both counselors at Green Pastures Camp in Grass Lake, Michigan. We married during our junior year after we transferred from Tennessee State University to Wayne State University.

When I met Kay, I had never been anywhere outside Michigan but Tennessee. After we graduated, I soon learned one of my wife's life goals was to visit six of the world's continents, which we did. She became my own private travel agent. Traveling was not only fun; it was educational. I give the biggest thank you to her for giving me the opportunity to see the world. Thank you, Kay!

Julius Armstrong, 68

Coordinator, Affirmative Action Programs

I WISH I COULD REACH UP TO HEAVEN

The word "thank," according to the Houghton Mifflin College Dictionary, is an expression of gratitude; one is grateful, appreciative when using this word. A number of wonderful, extraordinary, and loving persons who deserve my heartfelt thanks.

First and foremost are my parents, Lennie E. Stone, Sr., and Maude, who were great parents and excellent role models who laid the groundwork for my success in life. My extended family and my six older siblings showered love, support, and encouragement on me.

Beyond family, I am grateful to my community, Lamberts Point in Norfolk, Virginia, where I was nurtured from birth through college; my church family and Rev. J. Jasper Freeman and Rev. Bobbitt, pastors of the First Baptist Lamberts Point; and my first boss, Mr. Gonsulien at Acme Cleaners.

The principals, teachers, and support staff of my elementary school – J. J. Smallwood – deserve a note of gratitude, especially the lunchroom supervisor, Mrs. Long, and her staff.

I will always appreciate my baseball and football coaches, scout master, and mentors for their care and guidance.

I appreciate the principals, faculty, and staff at Booker T. Washington High School in Norfolk for their dedication. The high school faculty played a pivotal role in my life, and my counselor, Mrs. Dudley, insisted that I register in college prep curriculum and stayed on me to see that I achieved my best; other faculty members challenged me to set goals and achieve them. (In Mrs. Porter's history class in 1953, I met the girl who would become my wife of fifty years.)

Albert "Big Jim" Overby, the greatest football head coach, was my role model, teacher, and friend who recommended me to Coach Vernon "Skip" McCain who, in turn, gave me a four-year scholarship with total expenses paid to Maryland State College.

I am thankful for my college professors and coaches for their excellent teaching, encouragement, and support; for opening my mind and encouraging me to set high goals; and for going the extra mile in helping me to find employment after I graduated.

I owe special thanks to the director of the Detroit Department of Health, and to the Medical Technology Department at Herman-Kiefer for their excellent instruction and support; and to Herman Kiefer Hospital, which played a pivotal role in my life.

Lastly, my heartfelt gratitude to my wife, Oretha Hill Stone, our two wonderful sons, Clarence Jr. and Lennie James, Aunt Lucy and Dad James Hill for always supporting our family, and to Clarence and Kim for our grandson, Clarence Jerome.

"I wish I could reach up to heaven and
thank all of those wonderful worthy persons
who had an impact on my life."

Dr. Clarence L. Stone, Sr., 74

Retired Educational Administrator

GRATITUDE TO FRIENDS & FAMILY

1. Make a list of five family members or friends who helped to shape the person you are today. Pick up the phone and tell them how you feel, or send a card or letter.

2. If the individual is deceased, call out their name and thank them. Or, send their children or spouse a letter telling them how their loved one helped you.

PART III

GRATITUDE IN BUSINESS

Appreciate everything your associates do for the business.
Nothing else can quite substitute for a few well-chosen,
well-timed sincere words of praise.
They're absolutely free and worth a fortune.

Sam Walton

Businesses are challenged to renew their commitment to their employees and customers to create a culture that values, recognizes, and appreciates others in ways that express, on a daily basis, gratitude.

PERSONAL RELATIONSHIPS

We are caught up in a volatile, fast-moving world, where human relationships count for much more than getting along with the neighbors or having good times with friends. We live in a culture where the word "job" means an engagement that will last from 1.8 to 3 years, at most; where whole vocations disappear overnight, as they are outsourced overseas; and where it may take longer to find a job than one will hold it. In this mean world, your personal relationships may be all that you have and all that will get you through.

It begins with saying "thank you" to people who take care of you, of living your life in such a way that people will say in return "Thank you for all that you have done for me." You and they become one for the other and one for all.

Let us treat one another with compassion and empathy. We can afford to be patient; to hear out the other person; to take the time to persuade them that our argument is right; and to leave ourselves time to realize that they may offer the superior point of view on this day. And then say, "Thank you for talking this through with me."

As a business consultant, I see that nothing threatens an organization more than clinical depression, which is rampant from the front lobby to the loading dock. People perform work from, which they find little meaning, but as they actually are doing this work, they develop strong opinions on how it might be optimized. And yet too often there is no one in the organization to listen to their ideas; no path to bring continuous improvement up through the organization; no means to improve productivity and quality control and customer satisfaction in such a way that the whole organization might thrive and its constituent members might labor safe and secure. Rather than receiving a thank you, they are fired for trying to make things right. My job for over two decades has been to correct this deficiency with a long and impressive list of clients. They make a point to thank me when they see how much better this makes everything work. I get referrals, and my work is never done.

Thank you for the light that brightens the room when things seem at their bleakest. Thank you for creating a book that starts us on a return journey to civility by remembering that we each matter to the other more than anything else.

So, I wish to thank Dr. Gray, whom I have seen to be the most gracious exception to the rule in a mean society, the light that brightens the room when things seem at their bleakest.

Thank you for creating a book that starts us on a return journey to civility and good times by remembering that we each matter to the other more than anything else.

Lawrence Dolph, 65
Owner, Business Consulting Firm

WARM EXCHANGE

The valet attendant who parked my car became a little emotional when I thanked him for his service. He said that he had been parking and retrieving cars all day long with very little thanks. He shared that he had been laid off from work, his wife was expecting a baby, and he was doing his best to provide for his family.

Our warm exchange was touching, because two little words did so much for him and for me, as they provoked pleasantries and brought big smiles to his face and mine. A warm human touch of emotional expression goes a long way, especially for those who are in thankless positions and predicaments.

Lezlee Adkisson, 43
Social Worker

WHEN A SIMPLE THANK YOU IS NOT ENOUGH

A recent experience made me realize that a simple thank you did not convey the depth of the message I wanted to convey. At issue was the level and cost of my health insurance as a new employee. Soon after registering for that insurance, I learned that I was not fully covered. I phoned customer service and spoke to three or four different people, none of whom was able to help me. My next call was to Diane, a customer service representative in a different area. She listened to my problem, indicated she understood my frustration, and made a commitment to help me.

Over the next two weeks, Diane worked to unravel the cause of the problem, which turned out to be the hyphen in my last name. She worked diligently to align systems in several departments to ensure that my name was formatted correctly. Once the problem was resolved, Diane sent an email message detailing the problem and resolution.

I quickly shot back a one-word note: thanks. Later, as I thought about how great it was to have my problem solved, giving me increased benefits while saving me money, I realized I had responded inappropriately to Diane. She gave me so much, but received only a five-letter word in response.

While "thank you" and "thanks" are powerful words, capable of communicating gratitude, the way that the "thank you" is delivered is also important. Too often we are ready to complain loudly, using many words, but we shorten our response when all is well.

I researched Diane's chain of command and sent a note to her management, delineating her efforts on my behalf and complimenting her demeanor and poise. In the days that followed, I was pleased to see the outpouring of thank you notes to Diane from her entire up-line, as I was copied on many of the notes. Diane received the thanks she deserved.

Robin Wright King, 54
Product Manager

GRATITUDE IN BUSINESS

1. A business is developed or expanded by the efforts of a team, and the word 'team' has no 'i' in it. Think about your work team members (past and present), and thank them for their contributions to the organization before it's too late.

2. A good day's work is rewarded with a good day's pay. Tomorrow, commit to saying thank you to your team members or employees, and wish them a wonderful day.

PART IV

GRATITUDE TO & FROM TEACHERS

I am grateful to be able to create opportunities for those who came behind me. I ask only that they continue to be thankful for the opportunity to open doors for those who come behind me.

Earl Lloyd, 83

First African American

Professional Basketball Player in America

Other than our parents or family, teachers have great influence on our lives, not only when we are in our young, formative years but also later in life. A good teacher is worth all the appreciation we can give, for the lessons learned from them can last a lifetime.

EDUCATION IS THE KEY

Dear Coach Anderson,

I would like to thank you for providing me this opportunity to fulfill my dream of going to a university, getting an education, and playing football. Meeting you has changed my life all the way around. I thought I was going to have to settle for a full-time job at some fast-food restaurant, but now I see that God has something else in store for me.

You inspire me to want to do something greater than just flipping burgers or washing cars. I never saw it before, but now I see that education is the key, and I'm going to use that key to open up as many doors for myself as well as for others. I want you to know that I will bust my butt to get my degree and change lives, just as you are doing.

May God continue to bless you, so you can continue being a blessing for others as you have been for me.

Daniel Z. Gray, Jr., 20
College Student

WHERE WOULD I BE?

Morning, Mother...

I just wanted to thank you for birthing me and my twin brother. That must have been a lot, carrying two big babies at one time. Without you, where would I be? I'm not the best person, but who is? However, I'm definitely striving for perfection. I thank you; when others gave up on us, because we were a little active, you never lost faith or gave up.

Now, we're grown men, mentoring youth and letting them know that things will be okay. We will be graduating from college soon at the top of our class (dean's list and all). Wow! Amazing things can come when you put your best foot forward and have good parents behind you all the way.

Thank you, Mother. I will always do my duty as your son. You mean more than anything to me. Anything else I can do to uplift you, just ask. Always and forever.

Albert Allen, 21
College Student

CALL MY MAMA

Thank you: this two-word phrase is without a doubt the most used phrase in the universe. In every culture, in every country, on every continent, and in every language, there are words that translate to thank you. As an infant, even before I learned to say Dada or Mama, I was taught to say Ta-Ta, which in baby talk translates to "Thank you."

While thank you is a most common expression of appreciation for a kindness, be it a kind word, a kind deed or a gift big or small, the thank you that stands tallest in my memory was somewhat frightening.

As a substitute teacher in an elementary school, I accepted a week-long assignment in a fourth grade class. Harold, an energetic nine-year-old, was determined to convince me that I should not pursue teaching as a career. He refused to remain in his assigned seat. He refused to complete the assigned class work, and he did everything possible to disrupt the class.

On my second day in class, Harold became so disruptive that I grasped his arm and moved him to a desk at the very front of the class. Not wanting to be moved, he struggled and yelled, "Get your hands off of me. I'll call my Mama." At that very moment, the bell rang for lunch. While the rest of the class headed for the lunchroom, I led Harold to the school office and instructed him to call his mother. Sorry to say, poor little Harold suddenly lost his memory; he could not remember her phone number.

Following lunch, Harold returned to his seat at the front of the class. For the rest of the day, he did very little class work, but he was a little less disruptive.

On the third day, as I entered the school, a rather robust woman approached me. "Are you Mr. Hanshaw?" After making sure I had adequate space to escape what appeared to be a very angry lady, I answered, "Yes, ma'am. Can I help you with something?"

"I'm Harold's mama," she replied, "and for the past two days Harold did not want to come to school. When I asked him why, he said he had an old substitute teacher that made him do his work, so, Mr. Hanshaw, I came in to thank you."

A thank you that began as a somewhat frightening experience turned out to be a thank you that will linger in my memory for all of my days.

Renzy Hanshaw, 70
Former Teacher, Retired Deputy Fire Chief

A CONVERSATION

In the late 60s, right out of undergraduate school and in the year after the riots, I had the good fortune to teach at Webber Junior High School in what was then the highest crime precinct in the City of Detroit. Ironically I had organized a political campaign at that school two years earlier. The building and staff were scarcely older than the students. All of us were filled with hope, optimism, and the belief that all things were possible. The wisdom of the Vietnam War, whether the Detroit Tigers would be in the World Series, and which teachers were seen out together were the most talked-about subjects in the teachers' lounge.

I taught social studies to students in grades 7, 8, and 9. In grade 7, they looked and acted very much like children, but by grade 9, they left looking very much like adults. Class sizes were large, but the children were so eager to connect that each class period left you wishing that you had just five more minutes, so that you could reach another child or two. The days passed quickly. Semesters and young lives came and went in what seemed to be the wink of an eye.

It was an experience that I deeply loved but had to leave when law school seemed to be my logical next step. While my career path changed, the friendships endured. I think of my teaching experiences often. At a time when they seemed the farthest from my life, I received a phone call that brought it back to life.

I was in my office preparing for a court appearance. My assistant's voice came over the intercom, indicating Line 1 was an individual wondering if I was the same person who used to teach at Webber Junior High School. I took the call, and listened to the voice of someone who, in all honesty, my memory could not recall. I did not disclose this fact, as I listened to a former student, now a man and the father of adult sons of his own.

The purpose of his call was direct and immediate. He recounted a conversation that he and I had when he contemplated leaving school. Apparently, I discussed his plans for life. He had returned to our middle school frustrated by his experience down the street at the local high school. He told me that, as a teacher barely twenty-two years of age, I talked about life as I understood it.

He returned to school, obtained a degree, and pursued a lifetime career with one of the local car companies. He beamed about his three sons and wanted to credit me for all that he had achieved. I reminded him in an instant that I never took an exam for him, completed his homework assignment, or spent a day on his job. I never met his three sons of whom he is so obviously proud and for whom he is so grateful.

We agreed to have lunch to catch up on where life had taken us. I arrived at a local restaurant expecting a meal, warmth, and laughter that only old stories can produce. It was, of course, all of those things. Older now and so long removed, I wondered if I would still connect.

Two grown adults prefaced my name with Mister, as though class was still in session. The students, though, were now the instructors, as they both had stories they needed to tell. They came to thank me for touching and changing their lives. Yes, thank me, the twenty-two-year-old who was paid the whopping sum of $7,500 per year, and who always felt he learned more from them than he ever taught in return.

It was, as I said, a time of healing after a year of civil unrest when we all, black and white, yellow and brown, had to start over, to leave behind an ugly past. I wasn't the only teacher. We had thirty-seven of them per class hour and learned something from them all.

On this day, when they came to say thank you, I was the one grateful for the honesty, youth, and optimism; their willingness to listen to a new teacher scarcely older than they were. Thank you for sharing your remembrances, your good feelings, and success, but it is I who must say thank you, for I am a better person, a more enlightened one, who was touched by a love that I will cherish for the rest of my life.

Leslie Neil Greenwald, Esq., 66, Attorney

WHAT IS THANK YOU TO A TEACHER?

Teachers are many things to the children they meet each year. For some, we are the voice of authority, the knowledge bank of unanswered questions, and the one person who may or may not show compassion. Many times, teachers have stated that teaching is a thankless job. I beg to differ.

Thank you for this teacher comes in differently wrapped packages: an "aha" moment when the student finally gets it; a smile when they passed the test which they took unprepared; a hug for not telling Mom all the details of their behavior issue. But for me, a big thank you is when a former student, who struggled with reading and math in the third, fourth, and seventh grades, emails to let me know that she has arrived. She is a high school honor roll student with a 3.6 grade point average.

Making a difference and hearing about it is what thank you is to a teacher, particularly this teacher.

Brenda G. Flowers, 59
Fifth Grade Teacher

A LIFETIME OF GRATITUDE

When I hear "thank you," it brings immediate love to my mind. It is a courtesy that is lacking in our world today. Thank you to my parents, Willie and Thelma, who raised me to put God first, keep my word, and treat people the way I wanted them to treat me. Thank you to my teachers at Booker T. Washington High School in Montgomery, Alabama who taught me to excel in all of my educational pursuits. Thank you, Mrs. Josie Lawrence, for telling me I could be class president and not just a pretty face. Thank you, Mr. Clint Boswell, for teaching me how to file an income tax return. Thank you, Mr. Archie Moore, for showing me how a beautiful smile brightens those who see it.

I thank Mr. James Doggett, my eleventh grade English teacher, who taught me how to speak before an audience while reciting Shakespeare and to deliver each line of prose with precise diction and clarity. Thank you, Mrs. Reese (tenth grade English) for teaching me how to diagram a sentence and learn how to use all parts of speech.

Thank you, Mrs. Marguerite Elmore, who taught French and Spanish and instilled in me a love of knowing more than one language. Thank you, Mrs. Louise Spears, who was the head of the drama club. I still remember the staging of "Antigone" and hearing the screams of the ill-fated Tonda, buried alive by her brother.

Thank you, Miss Annie Larkin, who instilled in me an appreciation for the paintings of Degas, Renoir, and Chagall. Thank you, Farrell Duncombe, who marched our band into straight lines, pointed our toes, and led our rain-or-shine practices. Thank you, Mr. C. Smiley, our principal, who caught us sneaking off campus to march with Carl Lewis and the students from Alabama State and Booker T. Washington, and never told our fathers.

Growing up in Montgomery was a unique and loving experience. We loved one another as family and aided each other in times of need. I learned how to think and to be a lifelong learner from my teachers whom I love and cherish dearly. They were not paid exorbitant salaries, but they gave us something that money cannot buy: a loving, caring spirit that lives on in each of their students' hearts and minds. I honor Our Creator and live in a world where dreams are limited only by the perception of your thoughts.

Valencia Regina Shelton-Durham, 62
Teacher

GRATITUDE TO & FROM TEACHERS

1. We all had a teacher who impacted us in some way. Try to contact that particular teacher or their family members to share with them how this teacher affected you.

2. Teaching is a very unique profession that helps develop individuals in many ways, resulting in building and strengthening our society. Remember to teach your child to say thank you to a favorite teacher.

PART V
TOUCHED BY GRATITUDE

Kindness is the language
which the deaf can hear
and the blind can see.

Mark Twain

It is often the smallest gesture that goes unnoticed until many weeks, months or years later, when something reminds us of that kindness. It is never too late to express gratitude for the simplest act of kindness.

A VERY GOOD LESSON

A few years ago, my wife Brenda and I found ourselves with nowhere to go on Thanksgiving. Normally our Thanksgiving routine was pretty simple: friends would invite us over for the day, and we would be privileged to share Thanksgiving with them and their families. This particular year, Brenda and I made plans to have a quiet Thanksgiving at home; we were looking forward to spending some time alone.

She and I had often talked of spending our Thanksgiving some year at a facility dedicated to the care and shelter of people less fortunate than we were. As with most good intentions, there was always a reason why not this year. Now, we lacked a reason not to do it.

We called Grace Centers of Hope located in Pontiac, Michigan and asked if they needed volunteers for Thanksgiving. We were told that they had a full roster of volunteers for Thanksgiving Day, but they could use some help Thanksgiving Eve.

We showed up that Wednesday evening, received a brief tour of the facility, and went to the kitchen to meet the staff. Besides helping to prepare the dinner, we also served clients in a cafeteria-style manner. We prepared their plates and, in doing so, we interacted with each one.

The most wonderful aspect of the evening proved to be the interaction with the clients. In one manner or another, each one thanked us or shared a brief story and smiled while doing so.

After clean-up, as we were walking back to our car, Brenda and I talked about the fact that all the clients thanked us for volunteering our time. It was then that Brenda said, "We should have been thanking them, not just saying 'You're welcome.' What we learned tonight was the true spirit of giving thanks. The clients were just receiving some good food; we were learning a very good lesson."

Thanksgivings for Brenda and me have never been the same since.

Mike Ryan, 62

Logistical Business Owner

A LASTING IMPRESSION

One of the greatest life experiences I've had was at a convert meeting with our religious leader. He was a highly respected man known around the world. He extended me a welcome to the congregation, and throughout the following years, he always acknowledged my family and me with the same welcome, whether at home or in the community.

While our congregation was building a new facility for our growing community, our family hosted him during construction, as we lived very close to the new location. He would use our house when meeting with contractors or his board of directors, and we welcomed him for dinner and a much-needed rest. This time allowed us to have great conversations that were challenging and stimulating, that left a lasting impression on us and helped our children to become active members of the church under his guidance.

Apparently, that time also left a lasting impression on him. Once, many years later while still a leader of our congregation, he was seated at a table of religious and government leaders during a fund-raising dinner. As I walked by, he stopped his conversation and stood up in recognition of me and greeted me warmly with a (protocol-breaking) welcome. Within our religion, it is customary to greet women by placing your hand on your heart and slightly bowing. He thanked me by extending the same hand of welcome that I had done in the past by acknowledging me as just as important as those with whom he was sitting, and to bring awareness to the rest how he felt about my family and me. His expression of gratitude will forever be with me.

As our son always quoted, “What we do for ourselves dies with us. What we do for others and the world remains and is immortal.”

Mary Fontes, 64
Office Manager

AUNTIE JOHNNIE

Today was the day the Auntie Johnnie was coming home. Everyone was buzzing around the house trying to do their part to clean and cook to make everything perfect. Auntie Johnnie came to town only twice a year, but her visits were always special. When she wasn't there, she was always calling to check on us. She was like a movie star, and we had to be on our Ps and Qs to make sure we didn't say or do anything to offend her. She expected us to be perfect; she wouldn't tolerate anything less.

When the hour arrived, we were peering out from behind the curtains in the living room. We loved her, but we feared her. We were nervous as she exited the cab and approached the walkway with the driver carrying her luggage.

There it was... the long anticipated ring of the doorbell. We quickly ran upstairs instead of to the door. My mother yelled, "Get the door," but it was too late. We were hiding and peeking down the stairs as our mother opened the door and Auntie Johnnie entered the house.

Oh, my goodness! How beautiful she was! Just as we expected, she was perfect. She wore a gold cashmere coat and a gold and black hat, black gloves, and leather heels that matched her purse. When she removed her coat, she was wearing a gorgeous two-piece textured dress with a single strand of pearls around her neck and pearl stud earrings.

Then she asked our mother about us. "Where are the girls?" We took a deep breath and swallowed hard. "I have something for them." My mother called us.

We didn't answer. Instead we were wondering if we were dressed okay, if our hair was in place, if we remembered all the corrections she made to our grammar last time we talked. We weren't quite ready to face her. We needed more time to prepare.

Then my mother called us again. "Get down here!" This time we had no choice. It was a command performance. So we slowly went into the kitchen to say hello.

We embraced and kissed Auntie Johnnie, and she asked how we were doing. We replied that we were fine. Then she asked about school. "It's good," we said.

"What?" she said.

We repeated, "We're doing good in school."

"That's not the right word. Do you mean you're doing well?"

"Yes," we replied, embarrassed by the same mistake we made last time we had a conversation with her.

Auntie Johnnie is now gone, but this story illustrates how authoritative, proper, and classy Auntie Johnnie was. That was how she was raised, and that was what she expected of us. She exemplified success and respect.

Auntie Johnnie had high standards and believed it took a village to raise a child. She was instrumental in teaching us right from wrong in life. As children, we didn't understand her, so we thought she was strict, even mean. But she loved us enough to demand more, because she had a plan for our lives and only wanted the best for us. She knew the greatest boundaries in life are those we place on ourselves. She never wanted us to settle for second best; she pushed us to be better than we were so that we could become the best possible. She saw potential in us that we never knew we had. She knew accomplishments and achievements do not come without a cost. She expected us to work hard. She said "Plan your work and work your plan."

That's the key to becoming successful at whatever you want to do. It took us to mature to appreciate and understand that she prepared us for life's challenges.

To Auntie Johnnie, family was everything and education was a key component. Her strong belief in family and education was evidenced by her career choices and in the values and beliefs she instilled in us. She loved and comforted us whenever we faced adversities. She agonized out of concern for anyone she loved if things weren't going well. She often couldn't sleep if someone she loved had a problem. However, by morning she had a plan laid out to help solve the problem.

When our father died, Auntie Johnnie arrived from DC almost before we could drive from two or three hours away. She was by our mother's side, encouraging and holding her and us up. We know Auntie Johnnie loved us, because she took the time to help nurture and raise us. We loved her.

Auntie Johnnie's zest for education is evident in each of us and our children. By helping us, she enabled us, in turn, to help others. This was her version of "Each One, Reach One." We listened and heard her well. She left a rich legacy. Auntie Johnnie helped to define who we are.

In the words of the Negro spiritual, "If I can help somebody as I pass along; if I can cheer somebody with a word or song; if I can show somebody they are traveling wrong, then my living has not been in vain." Auntie Johnnie's spirit is preserved through all those she helped and touched. Her life was not in vain.

Even though we believe she knew how we felt, we waited too late to say "THANK YOU!" But, if she were with us, we know she'd say: "YOU'RE WELCOME!"

Carolyn Upshaw Royal, 59
Attorney

BEING PERSONALLY ENRICHED

The two most powerful words that have ever been joined together in civilized society are thank you. Saying thank you has transcendent, spiritual, and enduring qualities that allow each of us to make a unique connection to the lives of other people. No two words have ever given people more joy, respect, and honor than thank you. I have been personally enriched and have greatly benefited by being thanked and by thanking others who have played a special role in my life. It is from these perspectives that I offer my own thank you to those who have meant so much.

T **Thank You, God:** For breathing your spirit into this body made of dust, for giving me a purpose, for sacrificing ancestors, for loving parents, for exceptional siblings, for a virtuous wife, for grateful children, and for lasting friendships.

H **H**umility for every trial and triumph which has influenced my posture and predisposition for being thankful and saying thank you to those who have guided me along.

A **A**ttitude of gratitude which has greatly influenced the heights I have been able to reach in my education and career, none of which could have been done without the help of others. I am truly thankful and say thank you to those who have encouraged and believed in me along the way.

N **N**ew exposures, experiences, opportunities, people, insights, ways of thinking which have opened my mind to the magnitude and beauty of the world we live in. I am thankful for those who shared new information, and for new experiences that added depth and understanding to my life along the way.

K **K**nowledge of self, history, and culture that made me thankful for who I am, for my family and community, and I thank those who have inspired me and added to my knowledge.

Y **Y**ou and I are wonderfully and beautifully made, handiworks of God. Each of us has gifts and qualities that, if used as God intended, can enrich our own life and countless other lives in profound and enduring ways. We should be thankful for those who have made a positive difference in our lives.

O **O**ptions are available to choose the people, places, and priorities of life. I am so thankful for the vast array of options that I have to be anything I want to be and to do anything that my mind can conceive. I thank all those who have given good advice on all the options available to me.

U **U**nlimited possibilities which can be achieved, accomplished, and overcome when we say thank you to others.

Jeffery M. Johnson, PhD, 62
Male Mentoring Business Owner

THANK YOU

Thank you, Father God
For granting us your only begotten son
Jesus Christ

Thank you, Jesus
For your tremendous sacrifice of dying
On the cross and who got up on that
Third day with all the power in your hands

Thank you, Holy Spirit
For your divine presence in our lives and
Thank you for your divine protection of our
Families to keep them from all hurt,
Harm, danger and injury

Thank you, Mother
For being the vessel into this life
Thank you for your unconditional love and wisdom

Thank you, Father
For being the seed that fertilized the egg that became me
Thank you for your unconditional love and wisdom

Thank you, my Sister
For nurturing me along the way
For teaching me etiquette at God's table

Thank you, my Brother
For being a man to look up to
Thank you for teaching me how to read comic books

Thank you for the mountains' majesty
Thank for your reaching that mountaintop
Thank you, Brother Martin, for that dream

Thank you, blue skies,
Rolling brooks and apple pies

Thank you, Mr. and Mrs. Farmers
For your fields of vegetables, orchards of fruit,
Cattle for beef, and your milk o'plenty

Thank you, Teachers
For instructing our youths
Thank you for your patience and understanding

Thank you, Police Officers
For your honor, servitude and respect
In our neighborhoods and communities

Thank you, Sanitation Engineers
For keeping our homes and
Neighborhoods maintained

Thank you, DOT Bus Drivers
For your safe passage to our work and
Schools and home again

Have you ever seen the twinkle in a child's eye
When you say "Thank you" to them for
Giving you a hug and a kiss?

Thank you, Father God,
For blessing us with another sunrise
With another noon-day sun
And with another good night

Thank you cannot exist
In the presence of arrogance

"Please" is the preamble to "Thank you."

Reginald Broner, 59
Manufacturing Engineer

Margo Broner, 54
Research Analyst

A SIMPLE THANK YOU

Thank you is a genuine expression of appreciation and acknowledgment of service, love, kindness, and deeds. A simple "thank you" will empower individuals to extend themselves beyond physical, monetary, and personal well-being and gain.

Thank You...
...is like giving and receiving an embrace
...does your heart good
...can melt hostility
...can save and/or repair lives
...helps you to work/volunteer tirelessly without regret
...builds you up when you are falling apart
...can profit you much gain
...repays you for many hours of toil, struggle and strife
...says "keep on doing"
...has the power to heal and
restore a breach in a relationship
... and one will confirm their appreciation
of those two powerful words with a "You're welcome."

James West, 69

Retired Middle School Teacher

TOUCHED BY GRATITUDE

Promise yourself to locate someone that was good, kind, and helpful. Touch them with gratitude through a telephone call, a personal note, or whisper a prayer, if the person is no longer living. Even if they have passed on, send their family a letter thanking them for sharing their loved one in your life.

WHEREVER YOU GO, SAY THANK YOU!

Afrikaans – dankie *(dahn-kee)*
Albanian – faleminderit
Alsatian – merci *(mehr-see)*
Arabic – shukran *(shoe-krahn)*
Tunisian Arabic – Barak Allahu fiik
Armenian – chnorakaloutioun
Australian English – ta
Basque, Southern – eskerrik asko
Basque, Northern – milesker
Bengali – *(dhanyabaad)*
Bosnian – havla
Breton – trugéré
Bulgarian – merci, blagodaria
Burmese – *(thint ko)* kyay tzu tin pa te
Chinese, Cantonese – do jeh *(daw-dyeh)*
Chinese, Mandarin – xiè xie *(syeh-syeh)*
Croatian – havla
Czech – děkuji *(deh-ku-yih)*
Danish – tak, tahg
Dutch – dank u wel *(dak je wel)*
Estonian – tänan
Fidjian – vinaka
Finnish – kiitos *(kee-toas)*
French – merci *(mehr-see)*
German – danke *(dahn-kah)*
Greek – *(ef-har-rih-stowe)*
Gujarati – aabhar
Haitian Creole – mèsi
Hawaiian – mahalo
Hebrew – toda *(toh-dah)*
Hindi – shanyavad, sukria *(shoo-kree-a)*
Hungarian – köszönöm
Icelandic – takk
Indonesian – terima kasih *(t'ree-ma kas-seh)*
Irish Gaelic – go raibh maith agat
Italian – grazie *(gra-see)*

Japanese – arigatô *(ahree-gah-tow)*
Kirundi – murakoze
Korean – kamsah hamnida *(kahm-sah ham-see-da)*
Lao – khob chai
Latvin – paldies
Lebanese – choukrane
Lituanian – aciu
Malayam – nanni
Mongolian – *(bayarlalaa)*
Norwegian – takk *(tahk)*
Persian – mochchakkeram, mamnun, mersi
Polish – dziękuję *(dsyen-koo-yeh)*
Portuguese – obrigado *(oh-bree-gah-doh)*
Romani – najis tuke
Romanian – multumese
Russian – *(spah-see-boh)*
Samoan – faafetai lava
Scottish Gaelic – tapadh leat
Serbian – hvala
Slovak – dakujem
Slovenian – hvala
Spanish – gracias *(gra-see-us)*
Swahili – asante *(ah-sahn-the)*
Swedish – tack *(tahkk)*
Tagalog – salamat po *(sah-lah-maht poh)*
Tahitian – mauruuru
Tamil – nandri *(none-dree)*
Thai – *(kop khun kha)*
Tigrinya – yekeniele
Turkish – tesekkur ederim *(teh-sheh-kur eh-deh-rim)*
Ukrainian – diakuiu
Welsh – diolch
West Indian Creole – mèsi
Yiddish – a dank
Zulu – ngiyabonga

HOW TO SAY 'YOU'RE WELCOME' IN OTHER LANGUAGES

(Phonetic pronunciation in parentheses)

Afghani (teh-ah sha-MEL)
Albanian (fah-la-MEN-dur-it)
Arabic – àFowan
Australian – no worries mate (now wurrees mite)
Chinese (Cantonese) (mm ha hay)
Chinese (Mandarin) (bu kuh CHEE)
Danish – Selv tak (SELL-tock)
Dutch – graag gedaan (grog GEH-don)
Farsi (Persian) (kha-HESH ME-ko-nahm)
Finnish (oh la HU va)
French – De rien (deh REE en)
German – Bitte schoen (BIT-eh shern)
Ghanaian – Ye n'ase da (Yuh nah-see dah)
Hawaiian – A'ole pilikia (ah-O-lay pih-lih-KEE-ah)
Hebrew – Bevlakisha (bev-lah-kih-shah)
Hungarian – Nincs mit (ninch mit)
Icelandic – Gerdu suo vel
Italian – Prego (PRAY-goh)
Japanese – (DOH ee-tah-shi-MAH-shi-tay)
Korean – (tun mon-AY-oh)
Latvian – Lūdzu
Norwegian – Bare hyggelig (BAH-reh HEU-geh-lih)
Portuguese – De nada (Jee-NAH-duh)
Romanian – Cu placere (Coo plah-chair-ay)
Russian – (po-ZHAL-stah)
Slovak – Prosim (PRO-sim)
Spanish – De nada (deh-NAH-dah)
Swedish – Varsagod (var-SHA-gode)
Tahitian – aita peapea (ah-EE-tah PAY-ah-PAY-ah)

ABOUT THE AUTHOR

Rare people grace our lives and inspire us with their presence. E. Delbert Gray is one such person. Since he was a young boy, he has had a radiant spark. As a child he was funny and mischievous, but he also had high aspirations, was polite, gracious, and thoughtful to everyone he met.

People are always thanking him for something he helped them to accomplish: educational endeavors, finding a job, starting a business, or just providing encouragement to deal with life's challenges. Delbert has used his influence to help hundreds of people realize their dreams.

Delbert is well-known as a true professional whose contributions to the business community have been remarkable. He has been at the forefront of helping to shape policies and influence best business practices related to increasing economic development opportunities for people of color throughout the country. He is viewed as an astute, courageous, thoughtful, and visionary leader; generosity and kindness are at the core of his being. He is one in a million, a teacher, coach, administrator, board member, community advocate, church trustee, accomplished athlete, son, spouse, and father.

Delbert hopes that everyone who reads this book will feel inspired to act, to thank someone, and to learn from others the tremendous joy of expressing gratitude to others.

The book you now hold is a gift of love from someone whose life has been a ray of light and love to others, thanks to his daily practice of kindness.

–Sylvia Sims Gray PhD

CPSIA information can be obtained at www.ICGtesting.com
Printed in the USA
LVOW070746241011

251786LV00003B/1/P

9 781600 476419